From The Amazon Best Seller Himself
ANTONIO STARR

NOT AFRAID TO BE
THE WORKBOOK!
FIRST

FIRST GENERATION
MILLIONAIRE

Printed in the United States of America

Produced by First Generation Millionaires LLC
Atlanta, Georgia

First Edition 2018

ISBN: 978-1-7324380-0-2 (paperback)
ISBN: 978-1-7324380-2-6 (ebook)
ISBN: 978-1-7324380-1-9 (workbook)

Edited by: Candace Sinclair
Cover and text design by Antonio Starr
www.antoniostarr.com

WELCOME TO THE NOT AFRAID TO BE FIRST WORKBOOK!

This is where you will document your current position all the way up to your future self. I put this in a separate workbook, so you will not only have space to write, but even more space to grow. There is plenty of room here for you to take notes, answer homework questions, and at the very end, you will create your action plan.

Don't forget to use pencil so you can make changes and adjustments accordingly.

This workbook belongs to _____

Get it down. Take chances. It may be bad, but it's the only way you can do anything good.

—William Faulkner

Chapter 1 Notes:

Chapter 1 Notes:

Chapter 1 Homework

Here are a couple of questions you need to ask yourself. Write the answers and don't be shy. Don't hold anything back. This is a conversation with yourself, where you need to be extremely honest.

1. To start things off, I would like you to take a moment to write a short letter to your ancestors. In this letter, I want you to thank them for what they have given you that you will use to elevate your lineage. I want you to specifically mention what you will use in your journey that they are responsible for. It may be something in your DNA like height, wit, or even threatening good looks. Maybe you have a code of conduct that dates back for generations that will empower you to be great. Whatever it may be, write it in the letter.

   _____

   _____

   _____

   _____

   _____

2. Now it's time to write a letter to yourself. Here is your opportunity to be completely honest with yourself about where you are in life and how you got here. We will discuss where you want to go a bit later after you get some information from the book. Oftentimes, we lie to ourselves about our position in life, but this is not the place for that. This is your personal letter to you.

_____

_____

_____

_____

_____

_____

_____

_____

_____

_____

3. Becoming a FIRST means you are not FIRST right now, so you have a lot of changes to make within yourself. **Are you ready, willing, and able to make these changes regardless of how hard it may become?**

_____

_____

_____

_____

_____

_____

_____

_____

_____

_____

_____

_____

_____

_____

"If my mind can conceive it, and my heart can believe it, then I can achieve it."

—Muhammad Ali

4. As stated in the book, your belief system is simply the level of belief you have in yourself and what you can accomplish. **On a scale of 1 – 10, where do you rate the <u>current</u> level of your belief system?** Remember to be 100% truthful.

I'm Defeated			I Think I Can				I Know I Can!		
①	②	③	④	⑤	⑥	⑦	⑧	⑨	⑩

5. **OK, now take the space below to explain why you gave your belief system this rating.**

_____

_____

_____

_____

_____

_____

_____

_____

_____

6. Here is where I want you to list any limited beliefs you've ever had in your life. Any "I can't..." statements. List them on the left side of this chart. On the right side, next to each statement, I want you to list a positive statement.

Limited Beliefs	Unlimited Beliefs
Example: I can't afford to do that.	I can't afford not to do it!

In case you need more space…

Limited Beliefs	Unlimited Beliefs

"The biggest rewards in life are found outside your <u>comfort zone</u>. Live with it. Fear and risk are prerequisites if you want to enjoy a life of success and adventure."

—Jack Canfield

7. On a scale of 1 – 10, how content are you with your current comfort zone?

Not Content   Somewhat Content   Totally Content

(1)　(2)　(3)　(4)　(5)　(6)　(7)　(8)　(9)　(10)

8. Please take a moment to explain why and how you got to this level of content in your life. If you feel like something or someone is partially responsible for you being at this level, then explain that situation as well.

_____

_____

_____

_____

_____

_____

_____

_____

_____

"Resistance's goal is not to wound or disable. Resistance aims to kill."

—Steven Pressfield

9. Resistance from those around you can really make you want to give up on your goals completely. It makes you ask if this is all worth it. **What kind of resistance do you currently face?**

_____

_____

_____

_____

_____

_____

_____

_____

_____

_____

_____

_____

_____

_____

_____

10. Some resistance is from the enemy within, created entirely by your limited belief system. **How much of your resistance is coming from you?**

_____

_____

_____

_____

_____

_____

_____

_____

_____

_____

_____

_____

_____

_____

_____

_____

11. Motivation comes from knowing <u>WHY</u> you want the end result of being FIRST. You should tie your motivation to a person or a purpose. Whatever you write here must stay with you throughout this journey, because they or it is obviously very important to you. This is for THEM and NOT you. Never forget that. **Who or what are you doing this for?**

_____

_____

_____

_____

_____

_____

_____

_____

_____

_____

_____

Chapter 2 Notes:

Chapter 2 Notes:

Chapter 2 Notes:

_____

_____

_____

_____

_____

_____

_____

_____

_____

_____

_____

_____

_____

_____

_____

Chapter 2 Homework

Yep! More homework, but this time, we are working on putting your dreams down on paper. Answer these questions and watch your dream begin to materialize on the paper. We are also in the beginning stages of formulating your action plan.

1. **On a scale of 1 – 10, where do you rate your goal setting skills?**

   I suck   I'm OK   I'm a pro!
   ① ② ③ ④ ⑤ ⑥ ⑦ ⑧ ⑨ ⑩

2. **Do you currently have a dream board? _____**

3. **Will you commit to creating or maintaining a dream board?**

   _____

   _____

   _____

"Setting goals is the first step in turning the invisible into the visible."

—Tony Robbins

4. What is your main goal right now? (If you do not currently

have a main goal that is perfectly fine.)

_____

_____

_____

_____

_____

_____

_____

_____

_____

_____

_____

_____

_____

_____

5. List the top five sub-goals you must accomplish in order to meet your ultimate goal:

    I:_____

    II:_____

    III:_____

    IV:_____

    V:_____

6. Can you complete this sentence?

    I promise myself to stay _____, stay _____, but also to stay _____ at all times!

Chapter 3 Notes:

Chapter 3 Notes:

Chapter 3 Notes:

"You gain strength, courage, and confidence by every experience in which you really stop to look fear in the face. You are able to say to yourself, 'I lived through this horror. I can take the next thing that comes along'"

—Eleanor Roosevelt

Chapter 3 Homework

1. Write down your top three affirmation statements that you

   vow to live (or already live) up to daily:

   I:_____

   _____

   _____

   _____

   II:_____

   _____

   _____

   _____

   III:_____

   _____

   _____

   _____

2. **Write down what you have to lose by throwing your entire self into your dream?** (Remember, losing something or someone isn't always a bad thing.)

_____

_____

_____

_____

_____

_____

_____

_____

_____

_____

_____

_____

_____

_____

3. Think back on your childhood. I bet tons of things scared you back then that you now laugh at. Maybe you were shaking when you first rode a bike without training wheels, or you were terrified to walk to school alone, or you feared the monkey bars, or what about that monster in the closet? Those fears make for some funny stories now, huh? Seeing how you have overcome fears in the past without dying can inspire you to overcome fears now.

Write down a few fears you've overcome in your life:

_____

_____

_____

_____

_____

_____

_____

_____

_____

4. **How many of your fears did you make up yourself? How many were planted in your mind by someone else?** You don't have to answer that one; I just wanted you to think about it.

5. **How can those experiences inspire you on this new journey?**

_____

_____

_____

_____

_____

_____

_____

_____

Chapter 4 Notes:

Chapter 4 Notes:

Chapter 4 Notes:

"The human spirit is like an elastic band. The more you stretch, the greater your capacity."

—Bidemi Mark-Mordi

Chapter 4 Homework

1. The more creative, the better. **What are some creative ideas that you have to achieve your goals?**

_____

_____

_____

_____

_____

_____

_____

_____

_____

_____

_____

_____

_____

_____

2. Perfect practice makes perfect. **What are some things that you got really good at after practicing?**

_____

_____

_____

_____

_____

_____

_____

_____

_____

_____

_____

_____

_____

3. Every weakness can become a strength with practice. **What are some areas in your life that require strengthening?**

_____

_____

_____

_____

_____

_____

_____

_____

_____

_____

_____

_____

_____

_____

_____

_____

4. Challenges can be financial, personal, social, or even psychological. **What are some challenges you are currently facing?**

_____

_____

_____

_____

_____

_____

_____

_____

_____

_____

_____

_____

_____

_____

5. **How can you circumvent or beat these challenges?** List a few creative ways to overcome the challenges barring you from being FIRST right now. Hint: Pull from your answers from questions 1 and 2.

_____

_____

_____

_____

_____

_____

_____

_____

_____

_____

_____

_____

_____

6. Finish this paragraph: **Moving forward in my life, I DEMAND**

_____

_____

_____

_____

_____

_____

_____

_____

_____

_____

_____

_____

_____

_____

_____

Did you feel that? That was passion!

Chapter 5 Notes:

Chapter 5 Notes:

Chapter 5 Notes:

"If you are working on something exciting that you really care about, you don't have to be pushed—the vision pulls you."

—Steve Jobs

Chapter 5 Homework

1. **The vision of YOUR future self that you have in your head right now, draw it here.** (so what if you can't draw well. Do your best)

2. (Fill in the blanks) **My vision is being casted by**

_____, and not _____!

That's all the homework for this chapter. Do not leave this
section until your vision is casted on that page!

Chapter 6 Notes:

Chapter 6 Notes:

Chapter 6 Notes:

"When we least expect it, life sets a challenge to test our courage and willingness to change; at such a moment, there is no point in pretending that nothing has happened or in saying that we are not yet ready. The challenge will not wait. Life does not look back."

—Paulo Coelho

Chapter 6 Homework

1. Lack of resources is one of our greatest handicaps. It's not that the resources are not there (because they are). It's that most of us have no idea what we are missing. In this section, I want you to think long and hard about the resources you are currently missing. Write them ALL down right here. It can be people, finances, or knowledge. **What resources do you currently lack?** (There's plenty of space for you to come back and add more resources over time, because as you grow, you will learn what you didn't know.)

_____

_____

_____

_____

_____

_____

_____

_____

_____

2. How do you plan to acquire these resources?

_____

_____

_____

_____

_____

_____

_____

_____

_____

_____

_____

_____

_____

_____

_____

3. You'd be surprised how many people you currently know that can help you grow. **List the names of everyone you know who can help you connect with the human and informational resources that you need to connect with.**

_____

_____

_____

_____

_____

_____

_____

_____

_____

_____

_____

_____

_____

_____

_____

4. At no point do you ever want to rely solely on others helping you fulfil your dreams. **How can YOU attain these resources on your own?** (Think networking events, think online social communities, think city departments and offices.)

_____

_____

_____

_____

_____

_____

_____

_____

_____

_____

_____

_____

_____

5. How will you make all this happen with the funds you
    currently have?

    _____

    _____

    _____

    _____

    _____

    _____

    _____

    _____

    _____

    _____

    _____

    _____

    _____

    _____

    _____

Chapter 7 Notes:

Chapter 7 Notes:

Chapter 7 Notes:

"The only competition that matters the most is competing to become better than your best old self."

—Edmond Mbiaka

Chapter 7 Homework

1. Here is the space for you to brag a bit about yourself. This is your opportunity to list all your strengths. I advise you to get a little help for those close to you, because we tend not to recognize how innately great we are at times. **What are your strengths?** (Again, more space is being added for your growth.)

_____

_____

_____

_____

_____

_____

_____

_____

_____

_____

_____

_____

_____

_____

2. What parts of your personality will make you successful? In other words, what makes you as a person valuable to others?

_____

_____

_____

_____

_____

_____

_____

_____

_____

_____

_____

_____

_____

_____

_____

_____

_____

3. What areas of your personality need strengthening? How can you become more valuable to others?

_____

_____

_____

_____

_____

_____

_____

_____

_____

_____

_____

_____

_____

_____

_____

_____

_____

4. **Earlier, we casted our vision into the workbook. In this section, I want you to describe the avatar of your future self. List the traits, disciplines, skills, etc., that your future self possesses.** Do not hold back. This is your chance to lay out the absolute best YOU.

_____

_____

_____

_____

_____

_____

_____

_____

_____

_____

_____

_____

5. **Name the top three Postured Up people you'd like to emulate moving forward and describe why.** (These should be the first people you seek out to be your mentors whether in person or virtually through the internet.)

_____

_____

_____

_____

_____

_____

_____

_____

_____

_____

_____

_____

_____

_____

_____

_____

_____

Chapter 8 Notes:

Chapter 8 Notes:

Chapter 8 Notes:

Chapter 8 Homework

1. Evaluate your life. Determine the things you are willing to quit because they no longer serve you. **What are you no longer willing to tolerate in life?**

_____

_____

_____

_____

_____

_____

_____

_____

_____

_____

_____

_____

2. **OK, this one may hurt you a bit, because so many people we love are causing so much of the pain in our lives. Who must you quit and why must you quit them?** YES, write their names down!

_____

_____

_____

_____

_____

_____

_____

_____

_____

_____

_____

_____

_____

_____

3. To stay focused on your goals, you have to eliminate the other things in your life that are mere distractions. If it does not contribute to your vision, it needs to be cut; even if it's only a temporary separation. **List those needless hurdles, old dreams, bad habits, and useless endeavors in your life that you must quit in order to grow.** (Be sure to indicate why they must go, because the *why* is important.)

_____

_____

_____

_____

_____

_____

_____

_____

_____

_____

_____

_____

Additional Notes:

Additional Notes:

Additional Notes:

"Do you want to know who you are? Don't ask. Act! Action will delineate and define you."

—Thomas Jefferson

Your Action Plan!

OK, this is where you take everything you've learned from this book, and everything you've learned about yourself and devise your plan. As I stated in the book, this is an ACTION plan, so you must be fully committed to everything you write on the following pages. Be clear and specific on what you want.

Are you ready to commit? _____

Since you surely answered YES above, we can get started.

1. Write down your ultimate goal. Dare to dream big!

_____

_____

_____

_____

_____

_____

_____

_____

_____

_____

_____

For the rest of this exercise, you will focus exclusively on that ultimate goal. Once you achieve it, we revisit this entire workbook and complete these steps all over again for the next goal. And so on...and so on.

2. **Write down WHY you must accomplish this goal.** Find every

    source of motivation that you can. The legacy you want to

    leave, a better life, whatever drives you to want this.

    _____

    _____

    _____

    _____

    _____

    _____

    _____

    _____

    _____

    _____

    _____

    _____

    _____

    _____

    _____

3. **Now list three sub-goals that you must accomplish to reach your ultimate goal.**

Sub-goal 1:

_____

_____

_____

_____

Sub-goal 2:

_____

_____

_____

_____

Sub-goal 3:

_____

_____

_____

_____

4. Remember, your goals need deadlines. Deadlines are there to hold you accountable and to stretch your capacity. **Set a deadline for each of your goals below.**

My Ultimate Goal Deadline: _____

Sub-goal 1 Deadline: _____

Sub-goal 2 Deadline: _____

Sub-goal 3 Deadline: _____

Remember, a deadline is just a guestimate. You may hit your goal earlier than scheduled, but then again, it may take longer than expected. The key is not to get discouraged if one takes longer than the other. Make your deadline obtainable but challenging as well.

5. **Write down every action you will have to take to reach your goal.** At this point, you should have a clear understanding of what you have to do as an individual to reach your goals. Write, write, write. Think about it and come back and write more actions.

_____

_____

6. **Now, list what scares you when you think about reaching this goal**. (Leave a little space in-between each fear.)

Your Fears	Three Actions to Overcome the Fear

7. Draw a star by the real fears that very well may happen. Then, cross out all the fears you know are made up in your head.

8. For each fear with a star next to it, write down at least three ways you can overcome that fear, or work around it.

9. List the toxic people you have to separate yourself from right away. Next to each name, set a deadline for the break-up date.

Toxic People in Your Life	Deadline for Separation

10. **Now, list who you want to replace the toxic people with.** You can list names as well as the avatar of the person(s) you need in your life to reach your goal. Be sure to list the skillset they must bring with them. Think streamline here. Meaning, it's about the quality of the people, not the quantity.

Replacement Person/Avatar	What Skillset Must They Bring

11. Who will be your Pacemaker aka your Rabbit that you will

chase to victory, and why?

_____

_____

_____

_____

_____

_____

_____

_____

_____

_____

_____

_____

_____

12. List your top three virtual role models aka mentors who you
   can look up to in order to get motivation when you feel down.

_____

_____

_____

_____

_____

_____

13. **Create a three-step plan for what to do when you want to give up.** What actions will you take to make yourself feel inspired and encouraged again? Who can you talk to or turn to for advice or a simple kick in the butt to get back on track?

Step 1:

_____

_____

_____

_____

Step 2:

_____

_____

_____

_____

Step 3:

_____

_____

_____

_____

Look at all the information you have on those pages. That's what you call an action plan, my friend!

I hope you wrote it in pencil and left space for additions that may come along as a result of your efforts. Be sure to set deadlines to hold yourself accountable and to show your support team that you are serious about your goals.

No procrastination allowed!

I am very proud of you for completing this workbook. You now have what a lot of people unfortunately will never have in a concentrated format.

Information!

Please do not allow this information to go to waste. I'd love to stay connected with you throughout your journey.

Here's how we can do that:

Join my private **Not Afraid To Be First Facebook group** to connect with myself and other fearless history makers:

antoniostarr.com/fbgroup

I'll see you up front!

Antonio.

www.ingramcontent.com/pod-product-compliance
Lightning Source LLC
Chambersburg PA
CBHW051432090426
42737CB00014B/2932